That's A LOT OF CROCK!

That's A LOT OF CROCK!

BRENDA STANLEY

FRONT TABLE BOOKS

An Imprint of Cedar Fort, Inc.
Springville, Utah

ISBN: 978-1-4621-1196-1

Published by Front Table Books, an imprint of Cedar Fort, Inc.
2373 W. 700 S., Springville, UT 84663
Distributed by Cedar Fort, Inc., www.cedarfort.com

Library of Congress Cataloging-in-Publication Data on file

Cover and page design by Erica Dixon
Cover design © 2013 by Lyle Mortimer
Edited and typeset by Casey J. Winters

Printed in the United States of America

10 9 8 7 6 5 4 3 2 1

To my family and friends,
who have always been such gracious guinea pigs

"Slow but steady wins the race."

—Aesop

CONTENTS

PREFACE

As the mother of five children, including two sets of twins born twenty months apart, I've had to find meals that are simple and easy but also delicious. It does no good to serve something that your family doesn't like and won't eat. When my children were young and still living at home, the Internet didn't exist, and my sources for recipes were from a small selection of cookbooks and an expanse of ideas, suggestions, and help from my mother and grandmother. They were the MacGyvers of cooking. Nothing in the fridge? No problem. They could bring it together, and it was always a feast.

Slow cooking has been my salvation, not only because it is an easy way to prepare meals, but also because the method of slow simmering makes for some of the most delicious and satisfying dishes. Meats become tender, vegetables are stewed, and flavors combine and are brought together perfectly during the slow and steady cooking.

Working all day and coming home to the comforting and savory aroma of a meal that is ready to serve is heaven for anyone who is busy and still expected to provide a meal. Even now as an empty nester, I still use my slow cooker often, and when the kids come home for a visit, the slow cooker works overtime.

So sit back and enjoy the day as the trusty slow cooker does the work and makes magic in that popular ceramic pot.

—Brenda Stanley

A QUICK HISTORY
OF SLOW COOKING

The original version of the slow cooker began with the use of iron pots hung over a fire or buried in hot coals. The food was simmered for many hours. This was a great way to tenderize tough meats and dense, fibrous vegetables. It was also considered cost efficient.

The Naxon Utilities Company of Chicago was the first to manufacture a version of what we use today. It was originally called the Naxon Beanery. It was composed of a ceramic pot that was fitted in a metal pan surrounded by heating elements.

The Rival Company bought out Naxon in 1970. Just a year later, Rival took the concept of the Beanery and produced an appliance with a similar function called the Crock-Pot. In 1974, Rival also created the removable ceramic pot, which became useful in both storing and cleanup. The Rival and Crock-Pot brands are now owned by Sunbeam Products, yet many other companies produce their own slow cookers.

TIMELY TIPS

- **Unless** otherwise specified, always cover the slow cooker with a tight-fitting lid while cooking.

- **Don't** open the lid of the cooker to check on things. It takes 15 minutes to reach the desired level of heat again.

- **The** slow cooker should be between half and two-thirds full. Too much or too little food will affect the outcome of the dish. For meals that serve between 4 and 10 people, use a 5- to 6-quart slow cooker, which is considered standard size.

- **Thaw** meats before placing in the slow cooker.

- **Avoid** placing the hot cooker insert directly onto a cold surface or in cold water. The shock could make it crack.

"Slow down, you move too fast. You've got to make the morning last."

—Simon and Garfunkel

"Slow down and enjoy life.
It's not only the scenery you miss by going too fast—
you also miss the sense of where you are going and why."

—Eddie Cantor

PUTTING ON THE BRAKES WITH BEEF

Slow-simmering all day makes even the toughest cuts of beef tender and delicious.

Porcupine Meatloaf

Spicy Hamburger Noodle Casserole

Stuffed Italian Flank Steak

Smoky Barbecue Beef

Spicy Asian Short Ribs

Lasagna

Creamy Mushroom Steak

Beefy Country Casserole

Cowboy Casserole

Asian Beef and Oranges

Beef Bourguignon

Chop Suey Casserole

French Dip Shredded Beef

Brown Sugar Corned Beef

Beef Stroganoff

Hungarian Goulash

Grandma's Pot Roast

Hamburger Tater Tot Casserole

Chili Mac

Cola Pot Roast

Shepherd's Pie

Rolled Cube Steaks

Greek Beef

Porcupine Meatloaf

A wonderfully hearty meal with a touch of spice.
A perfect welcome home on a cold day!

1 (10.5-oz.) can tomato soup

½ cup salsa

¼ cup water

1½ lbs. ground beef

½ cup instant rice, uncooked

½ cup onion, chopped

1 Tbsp. Worcestershire sauce

¼ tsp. salt

¼ tsp. pepper

1 tsp. minced garlic

1 egg

Mix together the soup, salsa, and water. In a separate bowl, mix together the ground beef and all remaining ingredients plus ½ cup of the tomato soup mixture. Shape into a loaf no longer than the slow cooker. Place meatloaf in the slow cooker and pour remaining tomato soup mixture over top. Cook on low for 7–9 hours. Serve with the slow cooker sauce over each slice.

Brenda Stanley

Serves

8

Spicy Hamburger Noodle Casserole

The salsa gives this dish a flavorful kick.

1 lb. ground beef

1 onion, chopped

1 green bell pepper, chopped

1 (15.25-oz.) can corn, drained

1 (4-oz.) can mushrooms, drained

1 tsp. salt

½ tsp. pepper

1 (11-oz.) jar salsa

5 cups medium egg noodles, uncooked

1 (28-oz.) can diced tomatoes, undrained

1 cup water

1 cup cheddar cheese, shredded

Brown the beef and onion until meat is no longer pink. Drain. Place in the slow cooker. Top with the green pepper, corn, and mushrooms. Sprinkle with salt and pepper. Pour salsa over top and then place noodles on top of the salsa. Pour the tomatoes and water over all. Cover and cook on low for 4 hours or until noodles are tender. Sprinkle with cheese just before serving.

Stuffed Italian Flank Steak

Flank steak is full of flavor, and, combined with a smoky and savory stuffing, your family will love this meal!

2 eggs, beaten

½ cup Italian bread crumbs

1 (2-lb.) flank steak, pounded to ¼ inch

1 tsp. salt

½ tsp. pepper

5 slices bacon

1 cup Italian cheese blend, shredded

2 Tbsp. oil

2 (26-oz.) jars marinara sauce

Mix together the eggs and the bread crumbs in a small bowl. Sprinkle both sides of the meat with salt and pepper. Pat the bread crumb mixture over one side of the flank steak, leaving about a 1-inch border around edges. Top bread crumbs with the bacon slices. Sprinkle with shredded cheese. Starting from one long side, tightly roll flank steak using string or toothpicks to secure.

Heat oil in skillet and sear the stuffed flank steak in the hot oil until well browned on all sides. Transfer the meat to the slow cooker and pour marinara sauce over meat to cover. Cook on low 6–8 hours. Slice and serve with marinara.

Brenda Stanley

Smoky Barbecue Beef

I love this served on toasted buns and dill pickles.

1½ cups ketchup

¼ cup brown sugar

¼ cup red wine vinegar

2 Tbsp. Dijon mustard

2 Tbsp. Worcestershire sauce

1 tsp. liquid smoke flavoring

½ tsp. salt

½ tsp. pepper

¼ tsp. garlic powder

1 (3- to 4-lb.) boneless chuck roast

Mix together ketchup, brown sugar, vinegar, mustard, Worcestershire sauce, liquid smoke, salt, pepper, and garlic powder. Place the roast in the slow cooker. Pour the ketchup mixture over the top. Cook on low for 8–10 hours. Shred meat with a fork and then stir to evenly coat with sauce.

Spicy Asian Short Ribs

This sweet and spicy dish is perfect with rice. The meat is succulent and tender.

3–4 lbs. beef short ribs

½ cup soy sauce

⅓ cup brown sugar

¼ cup rice vinegar

1 tsp. garlic, minced

1 tsp. ground ginger

1 tsp. sesame oil

½ tsp. crushed red pepper flakes

1 cup carrots cut into 1-inch chunks

½ head of cabbage, cut into quarters

2 Tbsp. cornstarch

¼ cup coarsely chopped green onions

Trim excess fat from ribs and place in the slow cooker. Mix together the soy sauce, sugar, vinegar, garlic, ginger, sesame oil, and red pepper.

Place ribs in slow cooker and pour mixture over ribs. Place carrots and cabbage on top. Cook on low 7–8 hours. Transfer the cabbage, short ribs, and carrots to plate and cover with foil. Skim the fat from the cooking liquid and discard. Turn the slow cooker to high. In a small bowl, whisk together the cornstarch with ¼ cup of water until smooth. Whisk into the cooking liquid and cook until thickened. Spoon the sauce over the short ribs and vegetables and sprinkle with the green onions.

Brenda Stanley

Lasagna

A unique and easy way to make a family favorite.

1 lb. ground beef

1 (24-oz.) jar spaghetti sauce

1 cup water

1 (15-oz.) container of ricotta cheese

2 cups shredded mozzarella, divided

¼ cup grated Parmesan cheese, divided

1 egg

2 Tbsp. dried parsley

6 regular lasagna noodles, uncooked

Brown the meat in a large skillet; drain. Stir in spaghetti sauce and water. In a separate bowl, mix ricotta, 1½ cups Mozzarella cheese, 2 tablespoons Parmesan cheese, the egg, and parsley. Spoon 1 cup of the meat sauce into the slow cooker. Top with 3 lasagna noodles, broken to fit, and then top with half of cheese mixture. Repeat with 2 cups of the meat mixture, 3 noodles, cheese mixture, and one final layer of the meat sauce. Cover and cook on low 4–6 hours or until liquid is absorbed. Sprinkle with remaining cheese; let stand, covered, 10 minutes or until melted.

Creamy Mushroom Steak

So tasty you'll want to serve this with rice or noodles to soak up the gravy.

⅓ cup flour

½ tsp. salt

½ tsp. pepper

6 cube steaks

2 Tbsp. oil

2 (10.5-oz.) cans cream of mushroom soup

½ cup milk

Mix together the flour, salt, and pepper. Coat the steaks in the flour and shake off excess. Brown the steaks on both sides in hot oil. Place in the slow cooker. Mix together the soup and milk and pour over top. Cook on low for 6 hours.

Beefy Country Casserole

This dish combines traditional flavors into a delicious and hearty meal.

½ lb. ground beef

2 Tbsp. real bacon bits

½ onion, chopped

1 (8-oz.) can tomato
sauce

½ cup water

½ tsp. chili powder

¼ tsp. salt

¼ tsp. pepper

⅔ cup long-grain rice,
uncooked

1 (15.25-oz.) can corn,
drained

½ cup green bell
pepper, chopped

Crumble the ground beef evenly over bottom of a 3½-quart slow cooker. Sprinkle with bacon bits and then onion. In a medium bowl, combine tomato sauce, water, chili powder, salt, and black pepper; pour half over beef and onion layers. Sprinkle rice evenly over top, then corn. Top with remaining tomato sauce mixture, then bell pepper. Cook on low 5 hours or until rice is tender.

Cowboy Casserole

This recipe is similar to chili, but the potatoes add a hearty goodness.

1½ lbs. ground beef

1 onion, chopped

6 small red potatoes, sliced

1 (15.25-oz.) can red beans

1 (15.25-oz.) can tomato soup

1 tsp. garlic salt

½ tsp. pepper

Brown the ground beef and drain off fat. Put chopped onion in the bottom of the slow cooker. Layer with ground beef, sliced potatoes, and beans. Spread tomato soup over all. Sprinkle with garlic salt and pepper. Cover and cook on low 7–9 hours.

Brenda Stanley

Asian Beef and Oranges

This sweet and tangy dish has lots of flavor and texture.
A complete Asian meal in one pot.

2 lbs. boneless beef chuck, cut into ½-inch strips

2 Tbsp. oil

1 small onion, thinly sliced

⅓ cup soy sauce

¼ tsp. salt

2 tsp. ginger

1 small green bell pepper, sliced

1 cup fresh mushrooms, sliced

1 head bok choy, cleaned and chopped

1 (5-oz.) can sliced water chestnuts, drained

2 Tbsp. cornstarch

1 (11-oz.) can mandarin oranges, drained and syrup reserved

2 cups beef broth

6 cups steamed rice

Brown the beef in the hot oil. Place in the slow cooker. In the same skillet, cook the onion until tender. Add the soy sauce, salt, ginger, green pepper, mushrooms, bok choy, and water chestnuts and cook until bok choy is wilted, about 5 minutes. Spoon this mixture over the beef in the slow cooker. Whisk together cornstarch and reserved mandarin orange syrup in medium bowl. Stir in beef broth and pour over ingredients in slow cooker. Cook on low 8–10 hours. Stir in mandarin oranges. Serve over steamed rice.

Beef Bourguignon

Julia Child made this dish famous. Hers took hours of work.
Yours will cook for hours while you are at work.

½ cup flour

1 tsp. salt

½ tsp. pepper

4 lbs. beef chuck, cubed

3 Tbsp. oil

1 cup onion, chopped

1 cup mushrooms, sliced

1 cup fresh parsley, chopped

5 tsp. minced garlic

4 bay leaves

2 cups red wine vinegar

1 cup beef broth

Mix the flour, salt, and pepper. Dredge beef in flour mixture. Brown the beef in hot oil on all sides. Place the beef in the slow cooker and add the remaining ingredients. Cook on low 4–6 hours.

Chop Suey Casserole

This unique dish uses ground beef. I love the flavors and textures!

2 lbs. ground beef

2 Tbsp. butter

1 onion, chopped

1 cup celery, sliced

1 (16-oz.) can bean sprouts, drained (reserve ½ cup liquid)

1 can cream of mushroom soup

3 cups frozen peas and carrots

3 Tbsp. soy sauce

1 (5-oz.) can chow mein noodles

Brown meat in skillet. Drain and add to cooker. Melt butter in skillet. Add onion and celery. Cook until tender and add to cooker. Add the bean sprouts and ½ cup reserved liquid, soup, mixed vegetables, soy sauce, and ½ can of chow mein noodles and mix thoroughly. Sprinkle with remaining chow mein noodles. Cook on low for 6 hours.

French Dip Shredded Beef

Tender and with just the right spiciness, this dish can be served on a roll for French dip sandwiches or in tacos.

1 (2-lb.) beef brisket	1 onion, chopped
1 Tbsp. olive oil	½ tsp. salt
1½ cups beef broth	¼ tsp. pepper
1 tsp. garlic, minced	

Brown the brisket in the hot oil on all sides. Place the brisket in the slow cooker and pour remaining ingredients on top. Cook on low 8–10 hours. Remove beef from slow cooker and shred, using two forks. Skim fat from juices. Return beef to slow cooker. Or place on rolls and use the juice for dipping.

Brown Sugar Corned Beef

Corned beef and cabbage with a sweet and spicy twist.
It isn't just for St. Patrick's Day.

2 cups apple juice

¼ cup brown sugar

2 tsp. brown or Dijon mustard

1 (3-lb.) corned beef brisket with spice packets

10 small red potatoes, scrubbed

2 carrots, cut into chunks

1 onion, cut into 8 wedges

1 small head cabbage, cored and cut into large chunks

Pour the apple juice into the slow cooker. Mix in the brown sugar, mustard, and the contents of the spice packets, stirring until the brown sugar has dissolved. Place the brisket into the apple juice mixture. Top with the potatoes, carrots, onions, and cabbage chunks. Push all ingredients into the liquid. Cook on low 8–10 hours. Slice meat thinly across the grain, and serve with vegetables.

Beef Stroganoff

A classic that is creamy with the perfect combination of savory and tangy.

2 lbs. lean steak, cut in
½-inch strips

1 Tbsp. cooking oil

1 cup water

1 (6-oz.) can mushrooms

1 (10.5-oz.) can cream of
mushroom soup

1 (1-oz.) envelope onion
soup mix

1 Tbsp. flour

1 cup sour cream

medium egg noodles,
cooked

Lightly brown the steak in the hot oil and then place in slow cooker. Mix together water, mushrooms, cream of mushroom soup, and dry onion soup mix. Pour over steak and stir to coat. Cook on low 7 hours. Mix together the flour and sour cream and then stir into steak mixture. Cook ½ hour longer. Serve over hot cooked noodles.

Hungarian Goulash

*A traditional favorite that will fill your house
with a delicious and hearty aroma.*

2 lbs. lean beef, cut
into 1-inch cubes

1 onion, sliced

1 tsp. garlic, minced

½ cup ketchup

2 Tbsp.
Worcestershire sauce

1 Tbsp. brown sugar

2 tsp. salt

2 tsp. paprika

½ tsp. dry mustard

1 cup water

2 Tbsp. flour

2 Tbsp. melted
butter

1 cup fresh
mushrooms, sliced

Place meat in the slow cooker and cover with the onions. Mix together garlic, ketchup, Worcestershire sauce, sugar, salt, paprika, mustard, and water. Pour over meat. Cook on low for 8–10 hours. Turn the slow cooker to high. Dissolve the flour in melted butter. Stir into meat mixture to thicken it. Add mushrooms and cook on high about 10 minutes. Serve over cooked noodles or rice.

Grandma's Pot Roast

No frills, but always a favorite. This will melt in your mouth.

1 (3-lb.) chuck roast

1 tsp. garlic salt

1 tsp. pepper

3 cups beef broth

2 cups carrots, chopped

2 cups potatoes, chopped

1 cup celery, chopped

Sprinkle the roast with garlic salt and pepper. Place in slow cooker and cover with broth. Cook on low for 6 hours. Place vegetables in pot and cook another 4 hours.

Brenda Stanley

Hamburger Tater Tot Casserole

Kids of all ages love this fun and tasty dish.

1 lb. hamburger
(browned and drained)

1 (36-oz.) bag Tater Tots,
divided

1 (16-oz.) bag frozen
mixed vegetables

3 cans cream of
mushroom soup

Mix the hamburger, ½ the bag of tots, mixed vegetables, and soup. Layer the remaining tots on top. Cook 3–4 hours on low.

Chili Mac

Simple and simply delicious.

1 lb. ground beef, browned and drained

1 lb. elbow macaroni, cooked to al dente and drained

1 (28-oz.) jar spaghetti sauce

1 (16-oz.) bag frozen vegetables

Place all ingredients in a large bowl and mix well. Place mixture in the slow cooker. Cook on low 3–4 hours.

Cola Pot Roast

The cola not only adds flavor but is a great tenderizer.

1 (3-lb.) boneless beef chuck pot roast

2 Tbsp. oil

2 (16-oz.) bags frozen stew vegetables

1 (12-oz.) can cola

1 envelope onion soup mix

2 Tbsp. quick-cooking tapioca

Brown the roast on all sides in the hot oil. Place the roast in the slow cooker. Top with frozen vegetables. Mix together the cola, soup mix, and tapioca. Pour over meat and vegetables. Cook on low 8 hours.

Shepherd's Pie

This savory dish has all the flavor of the original—minus the crust.

1 lb. ground beef,
browned and drained

1 tsp. garlic salt

1 tsp. pepper

2 cups frozen peas and
carrots

4 cups mashed potatoes

1 (12-oz.) jar beef gravy

Place the ground beef in the slow cooker. Sprinkle with garlic salt and pepper. Top with the peas and carrots and then with mashed potatoes. Pour gravy on top of potatoes. Cover and cook on low 4–6 hours.

Brenda Stanley

Rolled Cubed Steaks

A delicious and elegant-looking dish with a tangy twist.

8 small red potatoes

6 cube steaks

12 asparagus spears, trimmed

1 (.75-oz.) envelope dry Italian salad dressing mix

Place the potatoes in slow cooker. Top each cube steak with 2 asparagus spears. Roll up and secure with toothpick. Place each roll-up seam side down on top of potatoes. Sprinkle dry salad dressing mix over all. Cover and cook on low 6 hours or until meat is tender.

Greek Beef

A flavorful and unique dish that is perfect
for sandwiches or warm pita bread.

2–3 lbs. boneless beef
chuck roast

2 tsp. minced garlic

1 (24-oz.) jar Greek salad
peppers (pepperoncini)

Place roast and garlic into slow cooker. Dump entire jar of peppers including liquid over it. Cook 8–10 hours on low. Shred meat with forks and mix with the juices in the pot.

PATIENTLY PINING FOR PORK

From chops to ham, this mild meat is perfect for combining with flavors during slow cooking.

Sweet and Savory Pork Chops

Creamy Pork Chops

Sweet and Tangy Pork and Kraut

Sweet and Spicy Bacon Pork Chops

Asian Pork Tenderloin

Creamy Ham and Potatoes

Sweet and Sour Pork

Caribbean Ribs

Honey Barbecue Pork

Peachy Pork Chops

Italian Pasta Sauce with Beans

Sweet and Savory
Pork Chops

The sauce will glaze the pork chops for a tender and decadent meal.

6 pork chops, about ¾ inch thick

1 cup ketchup

½ cup water

1 medium onion, chopped

½ cup brown sugar

1 (1-oz.) envelope dry onion soup mix

Brown the pork chops on both sides. Place chops in the slow cooker. Mix the ketchup, water, onion, brown sugar, and dry onion soup mix. Pour over chops and mix to coat well. Cook on low 6–8 hours.

Creamy Pork Chops

These tender chops are smothered in a savory and creamy sauce.

½ cup flour

2 tsp. salt

1½ tsp. ground mustard

½ tsp. garlic powder

6 pork chops, about ¾ inch thick

2 Tbsp. vegetable oil

1 (10.5-oz.) can cream of chicken soup

⅓ cup water

Combine the flour, salt, mustard, and garlic powder. Dredge pork chops in mixture and brown on both sides in hot oil. Place chops in the slow cooker. Mix together soup and water. Pour over chops. Cook on low 6–8 hours. If desired, thicken pan juices and serve with the chops.

Sweet and Tangy
Pork and Kraut

This delicious dish combines some unique and flavorful ingredients.

2 Granny Smith apples,
peeled and diced

1 large onion, chopped

1 (3-lb.) boneless pork
loin

¼ cup brown sugar

1 (32-oz.) jar sauerkraut,
drained

1 (20-oz.) bottle peach-
flavored drink

Place apples and onion into the slow cooker. Set the pork loin on top. Mix remaining ingredients and pour over top. Cook on low 6–8 hours.

Sweet and Spicy Bacon Pork Chops

Smoky flavor and so tender—this dish will be a family favorite.

6 pork chops, about ¾ inch thick

12 slices bacon

1 (12-oz.) bottle tomato-based chili sauce

3 Tbsp. brown sugar

2 Tbsp. Dijon mustard

1 (8-oz.) can pineapple tidbits, drained

Wrap each pork chop in 2 bacon slices to completely cover the pork chop and secure with toothpicks. Broil in oven for 5 minutes each side. Mix together the chili sauce, brown sugar, and mustard. Place the pork chops in the slow cooker and pour the chili sauce mixture on top. Cover with pineapple. Cook on low 6–8 hours.

Asian Pork Tenderloin

So easy and such amazing flavor—the slow cooker
will leave it fall-apart tender.

1 (2- to 3-lb.) pork
tenderloin

1 envelope onion soup
mix

1 cup water

½ cup red wine vinegar

3 Tbsp. garlic, minced

3 Tbsp. soy sauce

½ tsp. pepper

Place pork tenderloin in the slow cooker. Mix together remaining ingredients and pour over top. Cook on low 6 hours. Serve with cooking liquid on the side au jus or over rice.

Brenda Stanley

Creamy Ham and Potatoes

This wonderful comfort food dish is great for
an Easter brunch or pot luck.

1 (28-oz.) bag frozen
diced potatoes with
peppers and onions,
thawed

2 cups shredded
cheddar cheese

1 can cream of celery
soup

¼ cup milk

1 cup sour cream

3 cups cooked and
cubed ham

Grease or spray the inside of the slow cooker. Mix together all ingredients and place in the slow cooker. Cook on low 4–5 hours. Stir well before serving.

Sweet and Sour Pork

I love the way the sauce is infused into all the different ingredients.
Even the vegetables have a wonderful Asian flavor.

2–3 lbs. cubed pork

1 large onion, sliced

3 Tbsp. soy sauce

2 Tbsp. water or apple juice

2 Tbsp. cornstarch

¼ cup brown sugar

¼ cup rice vinegar

3 tsp. minced garlic

1½ tsp. ginger

2 cups broccoli, cut into pieces

1 cup sliced carrots

Put the pork and onions in the slow cooker. Mix together soy sauce, water, and cornstarch with brown sugar. Add rice vinegar, minced garlic, and ginger to soy mixture. Pour soy mixture over top of pork and onions in slow cooker. Cook on low 6 hours. Place broccoli and carrots in slow cooker and stir to coat. Cook another 2 hours. Serve over steamed rice.

Brenda Stanley

Serves
6

Caribbean Ribs

*The allspice gives these ribs a unique flavor
that is not your typical barbecue.*

1 tsp. pepper

½ tsp. allspice

1 tsp. ground mustard

1 tsp. salt

3 lbs. pork loin back ribs,
cut into 4-inch pieces

½ cup water

1½ cups barbecue sauce

Combine all the spices in a small bowl. Rub the ribs with spice mixture. Place in the slow cooker and pour water over. Cook on low 8–9 hours. Remove ribs from slow cooker and discard cooking liquid. Replace ribs in slow cooker and cover with barbecue sauce. Cook on low 1 more hour.

Honey Barbecue Pork

*Sweet and tangy—it will melt in your mouth
and have you coming back for more.*

1 (3-lb.) boneless pork
roast

1 medium onion, sliced

2 cups sliced carrots or
baby carrots

½ cup barbecue sauce

¼ cup honey

½ tsp. salt

¼ tsp. pepper

Place pork, onions, and carrots in the slow cooker. Mix together barbecue sauce, honey, salt, and pepper and pour on top. Cook on low 8–10 hours.

Brenda Stanley

Peachy Pork Chops

The unique combination of flavors will make this an instant favorite.

6 pork chops, ¾ inch thick

salt and pepper

2 Tbsp. oil

1 (29-oz.) can peach halves, drained and reserving ¼ cup juice

¼ cup brown sugar

¼ tsp. ground cinnamon

¼ tsp. ground cloves

1 (8-oz.) can tomato sauce

¼ cup vinegar

Season chops with salt and pepper. Brown chops on both sides in hot oil. Place chops in slow cooker. Put drained peach halves on top. Mix together sugar, cinnamon, cloves, tomato sauce, ¼ cup syrup from peaches, and vinegar. Pour mixture over top. Cook on low 6 hours.

Italian Pasta Sauce with Beans

A hearty and filling pasta sauce with a unique beany texture.

1 lb. bulk Italian sausage, browned and drained

1 (26-oz.) jar spaghetti sauce

1 (15.5-oz.) can chili beans

1 (15-oz.) can black beans, rinsed and drained

1 medium onion, chopped

½ tsp. garlic powder

¼ cup grated Parmesan cheese

1 (2.25-oz.) sliced ripe olives, drained (optional)

hot cooked pasta

shredded mozzarella

Place all ingredients except cooked pasta and mozzarella in the slow cooker and mix well. Cook on low 8–9 hours. Stir well. Serve over hot pasta and sprinkle with mozzarella cheese.

Brenda Stanley

CHICKEN—THE BREAST IS YET TO COME

So many different ways to use chicken: savory, sweet, spicy, or a little of everything.

Alfredo Chicken

Creamy Broccoli Chicken

Chicken Tetrazzini

Spicy Black Bean Chicken

Italian Chicken and Potatoes

Salsa Mushroom Chicken

Cranberry Chicken

Buffalo Chicken

Cheesy Creamy Chicken

Chicken Tacos

Raspberry Chicken

Apricot Lemon Chicken

Chicken Stuffing Casserole

Chicken and Dumplings

Mexican Chicken

Chicken Cacciatore

Chicken Parmesan

Easy Cheesy Chicken

Hawaiian Chicken

Asian Honey Chicken

Chicken Hash

Herbed Chicken and Red Potatoes

Alfredo Chicken

So easy, yet so creamy and delicious.

3 cups uncooked chicken
cut in 1-inch pieces

1 cup sliced mushrooms

1 (16-oz.) jar Alfredo
sauce

grated Parmesan cheese

Place chicken in the slow cooker. Mix mushrooms and Alfredo sauce and pour over top. Cook on low for 8 hours. Serve over cooked pasta or rice. Top with grated Parmesan.

Brenda Stanley

Creamy Broccoli Chicken

*Just four simple ingredients, but the mild flavor
and tender chicken is a pleaser.*

4 skinless, boneless
chicken breasts or 6
skinless, boneless thighs

1 (16-oz.) bag frozen
broccoli or 2 cups
coarsely chopped
fresh broccoli

1 cup milk

1 (10.5-oz.) can cream of
broccoli soup

Put chicken and broccoli in the slow cooker. Mix together milk and soup and pour over top. Cook on low 8–10 hours. Serve over rice.

Chicken Tetrazzini

I love the creamy, light flavor of this dish.

3 cups chicken broth

1 tsp. salt

½ tsp. pepper

1 cup fresh mushrooms, sliced

1 can cream of chicken or cream of mushroom soup

2 cups uncooked cubed chicken

½ lb. uncooked angel-hair pasta, broken into 2-inch pieces

Place all ingredients in the slow cooker except pasta. Stir. Cook on low 8 hours. Add pasta, stir, and let sit with lid on 1 hour. Stir and serve.

Brenda Stanley

Spicy Black Bean Chicken

Spicy chilies and tangy cream cheese make for a wonderful combination.

2–3 lbs. chicken breast
tenderloins

1 (8-oz.) block of cream
cheese

1 (15-oz.) can black
beans, drained and
rinsed

1 (15-oz.) can corn,
drained.

1 (15-oz.) can diced
tomatoes with green
chilies

Place chicken in the slow cooker. Put the block of cream cheese on top of the chicken. Dump in the beans, corn, and tomatoes. Cook on low 6–8 hours. Stir before serving.

Italian Chicken and Potatoes

A hearty dish with a zesty zing.
The potatoes add a unique touch to this Italian meal.

2 Tbsp, Italian seasoning

1 (12-oz.) bottle Italian salad dressing

½ cup grated Parmesan cheese

2 lbs. chicken, boneless and skinless, cut into 2-inch strips

3 medium potatoes, quartered

Mix together the seasoning, dressing, and cheese. Place chicken in the slow cooker and cover with half of the mixture. Place potatoes on top and cover with remaining mixture. Cook on low 6 hours.

Salsa Mushroom Chicken

An easy and tasty filling for tacos or burritos, or good served over rice.

2 lbs. chicken, boneless
and skinless (breasts
or thighs)

1 (10.5-oz.) can
mushroom soup

2 cups salsa

Place chicken in the slow cooker. Mix together soup and salsa and pour over top. Cook on low 8 hours. Use two forks to shred chicken. Serve in tortillas or over rice.

Cranberry Chicken

This combination of flavors is one of my favorites.
It is both sweet and savory and the chicken is moist and tender.

2–3 lbs. chicken,
boneless and skinless
(thighs)

1 (14-oz.) can whole
berry cranberry sauce

1 (1-oz.) envelope dry
onion soup mix

Place chicken in the slow cooker. Mix together cranberry sauce and dry onion soup mix and pour over top. Stir to coat. Cook on low 8 hours.

Buffalo Chicken

Spicy and perfect for a party.

2 lbs. chicken, skinless
and boneless (breasts or
thighs)

1 (17.5–fl. oz.) bottle
buffalo wing sauce

1 (1-oz.) envelope ranch
salad dressing mix

Place the chicken in the slow cooker. Mix together wing sauce and salad dressing mix. Pour over chicken and stir to coat. Cook on low 6 hours.

Cheesy Creamy Chicken

The perfect combination for a dish that defines the term "comfort food."

2 lbs. chicken, boneless and skinless (breasts or thighs)

2 (10.5-oz.) cans cream of chicken soup

1 tsp. garlic salt

1 cup cheddar cheese, shredded

Place the chicken in the slow cooker. Mix together the soup and garlic salt and pour over top. Cook on low 6–8 hours. Sprinkle with cheese and let cook another 5 minutes. This dish is perfect over mashed potatoes.

Chicken Tacos

Super easy! All you add are the fixins.

1 lb. chicken breast

1 cup chicken broth

1 (1-oz.) envelope taco seasoning

Place the chicken in the slow cooker. Mix together the broth and seasoning and pour over top. Cook on low 6 hours. Serve in taco shells, in tortillas, or over rice!

Raspberry Chicken

*This rich and flavorful dish is the perfect
combination of sweet and spicy.*

3 cups instant rice

6 cups chicken broth

1 (12-oz.) jar raspberry
preserves

¼ cup Dijon mustard

1 tsp. ground ginger

2 lbs. chicken breast or
thighs, boneless and
skinless

1 cup pineapple chunks,
drained

Mix together the rice, broth, preserves, mustard, and ginger in the
slow cooker. Add the chicken and pineapple and stir to coat. Cook
on low 6 hours.

Apricot Lemon Chicken

Sweet and tangy. This dish is perfect served over rice.

2 lbs. chicken breasts, skinless and boneless

1 lemon, quartered

¼ cup coarsely chopped dried apricots

1 tsp. salt

1 tsp. brown sugar

¼ cup orange juice

1 tsp. thyme

Pull the chicken breasts apart and place them in the bottom of a 4½-quart (or similar) slow cooker. Squeeze the quartered lemons over the chicken, and drop the squeezed lemon quarters in the pot. Add the apricots. Mix together remaining ingredients and pour over top. Cook on low 8 hours.

Chicken Stuffing Casserole

A full meal in one pot. This dish is satisfying, creamy, and delicious.

2 lbs. chicken, boneless
and skinless

1 (6-oz.) box stuffing mix,
chicken flavor

1 (10-oz.) package frozen
chopped broccoli,
thawed

1 (10.5-oz.) can broccoli
with cheese soup

½ cup chicken broth

Place the chicken in slow cooker. Place stuffing and then broccoli on top. Mix together soup and broth and pour over top. Cook on low 6–8 hours.

Chicken and Dumplings

This dish combines creamy, traditional ingredients with
just the right amount of homey flavor.

5–6 chicken thighs (or
2–3 breasts), skinless and
boneless

2 Tbsp. butter

1 onion, finely chopped

1 cup celery, sliced

2 (10.75-oz.) cans cream
of chicken soup

½ cup milk

1 tsp. poultry seasoning

1 (10-oz.) tube
refrigerated biscuit
dough, torn into pieces

Place the chicken into the slow cooker. In a skillet, melt butter
and sauté onion and celery until tender. Add soup, milk, and poultry
seasoning and mix well. Pour over chicken. Cook on low 8 hours. About 30
minutes before serving, place the torn biscuit dough in the slow cooker and
turn to high. Cook until biscuits are browned and baked through.

Mexican Chicken

*Tender shredded chicken that is smothered in
a spicy and slightly sweet sauce.*

1 (20-oz.) can enchilada
sauce

2 Tbsp. brown sugar

¼ cup water

5 boneless, skinless
chicken thighs

Mix together the enchilada sauce, brown sugar, and water. Pour into the slow cooker. Add the chicken and stir to coat. Cook on low 6–8 hours. Shred chicken with a fork while still in the slow cooker. Serve in tortillas with any of your favorite fixings, over rice, or however you like.

Brenda Stanley

Chicken Cacciatore

Rich and flavorful, this Italian meal will bring the entire family to the table.

2 lbs. chicken, skinless and boneless (breasts or thighs)

2 tsp. seasoned salt

2 Tbsp. olive oil

1 (16-oz.) jar spaghetti sauce

1 (16-oz.) can diced tomatoes

¼ cup dry white wine or chicken broth

Sprinkle the chicken with seasoned salt. Brown the chicken in hot oil on all sides. Place chicken in the slow cooker. Mix together remaining ingredients and pour over top. Cook on low 6 hours. Serve over cooked spaghetti or linguine noodles.

Chicken Parmesan

This traditional favorite is tender and full of flavor.
The only thing it's missing is the breading and frying!

2 lbs. chicken, boneless
and skinless

1 (28-oz.) can crushed
tomatoes

2 tsp. garlic, minced

1 (4-oz.) can sliced black
olives

1 (4-oz.) sliced
mushrooms

2 tsp. oregano

2 tsp. basil

1 tsp. thyme

1 cup shredded
mozzarella cheese

Cut the chicken into serving-size pieces and place in the slow cooker. Mix together tomatoes, garlic, olives, mushrooms, and spices. Pour over chicken and spread evenly. Cook on low 8–10 hours. Five minutes before serving, place a small mound of mozzarella on each piece of chicken. Cook until melted.

Easy Cheesy Chicken

Perfect for serving over macaroni noodles. The kids eat it up!

2 lbs. chicken, boneless and skinless

1 (10.5-oz.) can cream of chicken soup

1 (10.5-oz.) can cheddar cheese soup

1 cup milk

¼ tsp. garlic powder

Place the chicken in the slow cooker. Mix together remaining ingredients and pour over top. Cook on low 6–8 hours. Serve over noodles or rice.

Serves 8

Hawaiian Chicken

I love the sweet and tangy flavor of this dish.
The chicken is tender and coated with flavor.

2 lbs. chicken, boneless
and skinless

1 (16-oz.) bottle honey
barbecue sauce

1 (8-oz.) can crushed
pineapple, undrained

Place the chicken in the slow cooker. Mix together barbecue sauce and pineapple and pour over top. Cook on low 6 hours. Serve over rice or on buns.

Brenda Stanley

Asian Honey Chicken

The soy and honey mix for a wonderful flavor.
Served over rice, this dish is a favorite.

2 lbs. chicken, boneless and skinless

1 cup honey

½ cup soy sauce

1 tsp. minced garlic

2 Tbsp. tomato paste

¼ cup water

1 tsp. pepper

1 Tbsp. vegetable oil

2 tsp. sugar

1 tsp. brown sugar

1 Tbsp. ground ginger

Place the chicken into slow cooker. Mix together remaining ingredients and pour over chicken. Cook on low 6 hours. Use two forks to shred bits and mix with the sauce. Serve on buns or over rice.

Chicken Hash

Savory, spicy, and full of hearty flavor.

1 (28-oz.) bag frozen
hash brown potatoes

1 lb. ground chicken,
browned and drained

1 onion, chopped

1 (12-oz.) can evaporated
milk

3 Tbsp. steak sauce

2 Tbsp. yellow mustard

1 tsp. salt

½ tsp. pepper

½ cup shredded Swiss
cheese

¼ cup fresh chopped
parsley or 2 Tbsp. dried

Place the potatoes, chicken, and onion in the slow cooker. Mix together evaporated milk, steak sauce, mustard, salt, and pepper. Pour over chicken and stir well. Cook on low 4 hours. Stir and then sprinkle with cheese and parsley. Cook additional 30 minutes or until cheese is melted.

Brenda Stanley

Herbed Chicken and Red Potatoes

Lots of fresh flavors! This is the perfect dish for Sunday dinner.

2–3 lbs. chicken pieces
(legs and thighs are great)

6 red potatoes, halved

1 (6-oz.) can sliced
mushrooms, liquid
reserved

1 onion, sliced

1 cup sliced celery

2 Tbsp. butter, melted

½ tsp. paprika

½ tsp. minced garlic

1 Tbsp. minced fresh
parsley

1 tsp. garlic salt

½ tsp. lemon pepper

½ tsp. dried tarragon

1 Tbsp. soy sauce

½ cup water

Place the chicken, potatoes, mushrooms, onion, and celery in the slow cooker. Mix together the melted butter, paprika, garlic, parsley, salt, pepper, tarragon, soy sauce, water, and liquid from canned mushrooms. Pour liquid mixture over chicken and vegetables. Cook on low 6 hours. Remove chicken and vegetables with a slotted spoon. Cover with foil to keep warm. Thicken gravy by adding 1 tablespoon of flour mixed with ¼ cup of water, and then add to the slow cooker. Cook another 10 minutes until thick.

"The trees that are slow to grow bear the best fruit."

—Molière

CHILLIN' OUT WITH CHILI, SOUPS, AND STEWS

Is anything better than a steaming-hot bowl of flavorful hominess after a cold day?

White Bean Chicken Chili

Enchilada Stew

Chuck Wagon Stew

Creamy Potato Soup

Hearty Hamburger Stew

Chicken Chili

Buffalo Chicken Soup

Creamy Cheese Soup

Creamy Chicken Noodle Soup

Hearty Beef and Bean Chili

Beef Barley and Lentil Soup

Chicken Taco Soup

Spicy Split Pea Soup

White Bean Chicken Chili

I love this unique and flavorful chili. It's perfect for a stay-indoors meal.

4 chicken breasts

3 (15-oz.) cans great
northern beans,
undrained

1 (16-oz.) jar salsa

2 cups Monterey Jack
cheese, shredded

Place the chicken in the slow cooker. Add the beans and the salsa. Cook on low 8 hours. Remove the chicken to a large bowl and shred with two forks. Return to the slow cooker. Add the cheese and stir. Cook another 5 minutes or until cheese is melted.

Brenda Stanley

Enchilada Stew

*This easy stew combines Mexican spice into
a creamy and delicious soup.*

1 lb. ground beef

1 medium onion,
chopped

1 (4.5-oz.) can chopped
chilies

1 (16-oz.) can enchilada
sauce

1 (10.5-oz.) can golden
mushroom soup

1 (10.5-oz.) can cheddar
cheese soup

1 (10.5-oz.) can cream of
mushroom soup

1 (10.5-oz.) can cream of
celery soup

1 bag tortilla chips,
coarsely crushed

Brown the hamburger and onion. Drain. Place all ingredients in
the slow cooker except chips. Stir well and cook low 4–6 hours. Stir
in chips 15 minutes before you are ready to eat.

Chuck Wagon Stew

*Thick and tasty, this stew is a main dish
that will satisfy even the heartiest of appetites.*

½ cup Italian bread crumbs

1 tsp. salt

1 tsp. pepper

2 lbs. beef chuck, trimmed and cut into 1-inch cubes

1 medium onion, chopped

1 cup sliced carrots

1 cup chopped celery

1 (4.5-oz.) can sliced mushrooms, drained

1 tsp. dried basil

⅓ cup quick-cooking tapioca

1 tsp. soy sauce

2 (10.5-oz.) cans tomato soup

1 cup beef broth

Mix together the bread crumbs, salt, and pepper and toss with beef cubes. Place the beef into the slow cooker and add onion, carrots, celery, and mushrooms. Mix together the basil, tapioca, soy sauce, tomato soup, and broth. Pour mixture over all. Cook on low 10 hours. Stir before serving.

Brenda Stanley

Creamy Potato Soup

Few things in life are as comforting as this succulent and tasty soup.

8 cups diced potatoes

½ cup chopped onion

5½ cups chicken broth

1 can cream of chicken soup

½ tsp. pepper

1 (8-oz.) brick cream cheese, cubed

½ cup real bacon bits

snipped chives (optional)

Place the first 5 ingredients into the slow cooker and mix well. Cook on low 8–10 hours. Add cream cheese and stir until well blended. Serve topped with bacon bits and chives.

Hearty Hamburger Stew

A twist on a classic favorite.

1 lb. ground beef,
browned and drained

4 potatoes, peeled and
cubed

2 cups baby carrots

3 cups water

1 (1-oz.) envelope dry
onion soup mix

1 tsp. garlic powder

1 tsp. Italian seasoning

1 tsp. salt

½ tsp. pepper

1 (10.5-oz.) can tomato
soup

1 (6-oz.) can tomato
paste

Place the ground beef, potatoes, and carrots in the slow cooker and stir. Mix the water, dry soup mix, and spices and pour over top. Stir well. Cook on low 6–8 hours. Stir in soup and tomato paste. Cook 1 hour or until heated through.

Chicken Chili

Not too spicy, and the chicken is fall-apart tender.

1 (15.25-oz.) can black beans, drained and rinsed

1 (15.25-oz.) can kidney beans, drained and rinsed

1 (15.25-oz.) can corn, drained

2 cups tomato sauce

1 (28-oz.) can diced tomatoes

1 (1-oz.) envelope taco seasoning

1 Tbsp. chili powder

2 lbs. chicken, cut in 1-inch cubes

Mix all ingredients in the slow cooker. Cook on low 8–10 hours.

Buffalo Chicken Soup

Spicy yet creamy, this soup will satisfy.

6 cups milk

3 (10.5-oz.) cans cream of chicken soup

3 cups shredded cooked chicken

1 cup sour cream

¼ cup hot pepper sauce

Mix together all ingredients and place in the slow cooker. Cook on low 4 hours.

Creamy Cheese Soup

So creamy and full of cheesy flavor.

5½ cups chicken broth

1 small onion, peeled and chopped

½ cup peeled and chopped carrots

½ cup chopped celery

¼ cup chopped red bell pepper

2 Tbsp. butter

1 tsp. salt

½ tsp. pepper

⅓ cup flour

½ cup water

1 (8-oz.) brick cream cheese, cubed and softened

2 cups shredded cheddar cheese

1½ cups water

Mix together the first 8 ingredients in the slow cooker. Cover and cook on low 7–8 hours. Mix together the flour and ½ cup water until smooth. Stir into soup. Cook on high 30 more minutes or until soup is thickened. Stir in cream cheese, cheddar cheese, and 1½ cups water. Cook on low another 15 minutes or until heated through.

Creamy Chicken Noodle Soup

This creamy, decadent version of an old favorite will have everyone wanting seconds.

5 cups water

1 (10.5-oz.) can cream of chicken soup

1 (10.5-oz.) can cream of mushroom soup

2 cups cooked and chopped chicken

2 cups frozen peas and carrots

1 tsp. lemon pepper

1 tsp. salt

1½ cups egg noodles, uncooked

Mix together the water and soups in the slow cooker. Add the chicken, vegetables, pepper, and salt. Mix well. Cook on low 6 hours. Turn slow cooker to high and stir in the noodles. Cook another 30 minutes or until noodles are tender.

Brenda Stanley

Hearty Beef and Bean Chili

A classic chili that will fill the house with a spicy aroma.

1½ lbs. ground beef, browned and drained

1 large onion, chopped

2 tsp. minced garlic

1 (10.5-oz.) can tomato soup

1 (14.5-oz.) can diced tomatoes

½ cup water

2 (15-oz.) cans kidney beans, drained and rinsed

¼ cup chili powder

2 tsp. ground cumin

Mix together all ingredients in the slow cooker. Cook on low 8 hours.

Beef Barley and Lentil Soup

This soup is super hearty and full of flavor. It is definitely a meal in itself.

1 lb. ground beef

1 medium onion, chopped

2 cups cubed red potatoes

1 cup chopped celery

1 cup chopped carrots

1 cup dry lentils, rinsed

½ cup medium pearl barley

8 cups water

2 tsp. beef bouillon granules

1 tsp. salt

½ tsp. lemon pepper

2 (14.5-oz.) cans stewed tomatoes

Brown the beef and onion until beef is no longer pink. Drain. Place meat and onion into the slow cooker. Place in layers the potatoes, celery, carrots, lentils, and barley. Mix together the water, bouillon, salt, and lemon pepper. Pour over everything in slow cooker. Cook on low 6 hours or until vegetables and barley are tender. Add the tomatoes. Stir and cook another 2 hours.

Brenda Stanley

Chicken Taco Soup

Feel the heat from this spicy soup. It's the perfect way to warm you up.

1 onion, chopped

1 (16-oz.) can chili beans

1 (15-oz.) can black beans, drained and rinsed

1 (15-oz.) can corn, drained

1 (8-oz.) can tomato sauce

1½ cups chicken broth

2 (10-oz.) cans diced tomatoes with green chilies, undrained

1 (1.25-oz.) packet taco seasoning

3 whole chicken breasts, skinless and boneless

cheddar cheese, shredded

sour cream

tortilla chips, crushed

Place the onion, chili beans, black beans, corn, tomato sauce, broth, and diced tomatoes in the slow cooker. Add taco seasoning, and stir to blend. Place the chicken breasts on top of the mixture, pressing down slightly until just covered by the other ingredients. Cook on low 5 hours. Remove chicken breasts from slow cooker and place in a large bowl. Shred using two forks and then return to slow cooker and stir. Continue cooking 2 hours. Serve topped with cheese, sour cream, and chips.

Spicy Split Pea Soup

This is a spicy, zingy version of everyone's favorite winter soup.

1 cup chopped carrots

2 Tbsp. chopped garlic

1 cup chopped celery

2 medium onions, chopped

2 cups shredded cabbage

1 Tbsp. olive oil

1 cube vegetable bouillon

10 cups water

2 cups split green peas

1 tsp. thyme

1 tsp. oregano

¼ tsp. sage

¼ tsp. celery seed

1 tsp. basil

1 tsp. marjoram

1 tsp. seasoned salt

1 jalapeño pepper, chopped

Turn the slow cooker to high. Sauté the first 5 ingredients in oil for 10 minutes in bottom of the slow cooker until a bit glazed. Mix in the remaining ingredients. Heat until pot is bubbling, and then turn heat to low. Cook 2–3 hours.

SAVORING THE SIDES

Think slow cooking is only for main dishes? Think again.
Flavorful side dishes are perfect for simple meals that need a little kick.

Savory and Saucy
Green Beans

Cheesy Broccoli and
Cauliflower

Cabbage and Apple
Casserole

Orange-Glazed Carrots

Pineapple Cinnamon
Squash

Candied Yams and
Cranberries

Apple-Filled Squash

Lemony Steamed
Artichokes

Cream Cheese Corn

Spinach and Artichoke
Dip

Old-Fashioned Baked
Beans

Cheesy Potatoes with a
Twist

Savory and Saucy Green Beans

The crispness of the fresh green beans mixed with the spices really sets this dish apart.

1 lb. fresh green beans

1 (28-oz.) can crushed tomatoes

2 Tbsp. crumbled bacon

2 tsp. minced garlic

1 tsp. dried rosemary

⅛ tsp. freshly ground black pepper

Mix together all ingredients in the slow cooker. Cook on low 5–7 hours.

Brenda Stanley

Cheesy Broccoli and Cauliflower

So creamy and cheesy with just a touch of bacon.

2 cups broccoli cut into bite-sized pieces

2 cups cauliflower cut into bite-sized pieces

salt and pepper to taste

1 (10.5-oz.) can nacho cheese soup

1 cup water

¼ cup crumbled bacon

Place broccoli and cauliflower in the slow cooker. Sprinkle with salt and pepper. Mix together the soup and water. Pour soup over top and stir to coat. Sprinkle with bacon. Cook on low 4–6 hours.

Cabbage and Apple Casserole

Hearty and delicious, this could work as a light meal.

2 Tbsp. butter

2 onions, chopped

1 small cabbage, shredded, or 1 bag shredded cabbage

2 Granny Smith apples, thinly sliced

2 tsp. cider vinegar

2 Tbsp. sugar

1 tsp. salt

½ tsp. pepper

2 cups chicken broth

½ cup mashed potatoes

Sauté the onion in the butter until tender. In the slow cooker, place alternating layers of cabbage and then a layer of apples. Add the onion. Mix together the vinegar, sugar, salt, and pepper. Pour mixture over the top. Whisk the broth into the mashed potatoes and pour it over the cabbage. Cook on high 3–4 hours

Orange-Glazed Carrots

Sweet and tangy—a wonderful side dish for steak and potatoes.

4 cups sliced carrots

1 tsp. salt

½ cup maple syrup

¼ cup butter, melted

¾ cup orange juice

Place the carrots in the slow cooker and sprinkle with salt. Mix together the syrup, butter, and orange juice and pour over top of carrots. Stir to combine. Cook on low 6–8 hours.

Pineapple Cinnamon Squash

Autumn is in the air when this dish is served.
Such a sweet and tasty side dish.

3 lbs. Hubbard squash or
banana squash, peeled
and cubed

1 (8-oz.) can crushed
pineapple

½ tsp. ground cinnamon

⅓ cup brown sugar

1 Tbsp. butter, cut into
small pieces

Place the squash in the slow cooker. Mix the other ingredients together and pour on top. Stir to coat. Cook on low 6–8 hours, or until squash is tender.

Candied Yams and Cranberries

My two favorite Thanksgiving side dishes combined into one.
A wonderful flavor mixture perfect any time of the year!

6 medium yams or sweet
potatoes, peeled and
sliced

½ cup butter

¾ cup brown sugar

1 tsp. salt

½ tsp. pepper

2 cups fresh cranberries

Place yams in a well-greased or buttered slow cooker. Mix together butter, brown sugar, salt, and pepper. Spoon mixture on top of yams and stir to coat. Place cranberries on top. Cook on low 4–6 hours.

Apple-Filled Squash

Acorn squash is buttery and perfect for using with fall fruits and spices.

2 small acorn squash, halved and seeds removed

½ tsp. salt

2 apples, peeled and chopped

½ cup brown sugar

½ tsp. nutmeg

½ tsp. cinnamon

1 Tbsp. lemon juice

4 Tbsp. butter or margarine

1 cup water

Sprinkle the squash with salt. Divide chopped apples evenly among the squash halves. Sprinkle each half with about 2 tablespoons brown sugar, a dash of nutmeg or cinnamon, and a few drops of lemon juice. Dot each half with 1 tablespoon butter. Wrap each squash half securely in foil. Pour water into the slow cooker. Stack the squash, cut side up, in cooker. Cook on low 5 hours.

Brenda Stanley

Serves

4

Lemony
Steamed Artichokes

I love how tender and flavorful these turn out.
The lemon juice gives them just the right tanginess.

2 cups boiling water

2 tsp. salt

8 peppercorns

2 stalks celery, cut up

¼ cup lemon juice

4 artichokes, stalks and
tough leaves removed

Combine the water, salt, peppercorns, celery, and lemon juice in the slow cooker. Place artichokes stalk side down in the slow cooker. Cook on high 4–5 hours.

Cream Cheese Corn

*This creamy and succulent dish will easily become
the main attraction of the meal.*

2 (16-oz.) bags frozen
corn

2 (3-oz.) blocks cream
cheese

½ cup butter

1 tsp. sugar

1 tsp. salt

½ tsp. pepper

Mix together all ingredients and place in the slow cooker. Cook on
high 2 hours. Stir every half hour.

Brenda Stanley

Spinach and Artichoke Dip

*This popular appetizer can be served right from the pot,
keeping it warm and tasty.*

2 (8-oz.) blocks of
cream cheese, at room
temperature

1 cup half-and-half

1 Tbsp. diced onion

1 tsp. minced garlic

½ cup grated Parmesan
cheese

1 (10-oz.) package frozen
cut spinach, thawed and
drained

1 cup drained and
chopped marinated
artichoke hearts

⅔ cup shredded
Monterey Jack cheese

Mix together cream cheese and half-and-half in a bowl until smooth. Add the remaining ingredients and stir well. Place in the slow cooker. Cook on high 2 hours. Stir before serving.

Old-Fashioned Baked Beans

This is the way baked beans should taste—
rich and thick and full of sweet, savory flavor.

2 lbs. dry navy beans

½ lb. bacon, chopped

1 large onion, chopped

1 cup molasses

2 tsp. salt

¼ tsp. pepper

¼ cup brown sugar

Put all the ingredients into the slow cooker and add just enough water to cover. Soak overnight, at least 12 hours. In the morning, cook on low 6–8 hours or until beans are soft and glazed with sauce.

Brenda Stanley

Cheesy Potatoes
with a Twist

*This is not your typical scalloped potatoes. The unique
cheese makes it extra special.*

6 slices bacon, chopped

4 large potatoes, peeled
and thinly sliced

½ cup grated Gruyère
cheese

1 tsp. salt

½ tsp. pepper

1½ cups heavy cream

Cook the bacon and drain. Place alternating layers of ¼ of the potatoes, ¼ of the bacon, and ¼ of the cheese. Sprinkle each layer of potatoes with salt and pepper. Pour the cream over all the layers. Cook on low about 8 hours.

"Many a genius has been slow of growth. Oaks that flourish for a thousand years do not spring up into beauty like a reed."

—George Henry Lewes

LAID-BACK BREAKFASTS & DAYDREAMY DESSERTS

The perfect beginning or ending to a nice slow day.

Four-Ingredient Breakfast Casserole

Sausage and Tots

Overnight Oatmeal

Florentine Breakfast Casserole

Eggs, Ham, and Hash Browns

Apple Pudding Cake

Cherry Crisp

Lemon Sponge

Baked Apples

Pineapple Upside-Down Cake

Apple Crisp Crunch

Berry Bread Pudding

Creamy Rice Pudding

Hot Fudge Cake

Four-Ingredient Breakfast Casserole

This dish may only have four ingredients, but the taste is savory and delicious.

1 lb. mild bulk sausage

1 (32-oz.) bag frozen
hash browns

2 cups shredded
cheddar cheese

10 eggs

Brown and crumble the sausage. Drain. Place ⅓ of the hash browns in the bottom of the slow cooker followed by ⅓ of the cheese and topped with ⅓ of the sausage. Repeat the layers. Pour the eggs over top. Cook on low 8–10 hours.

Sausage and Tots

This is a favorite for everyone in my family.

14 sausage links

½ (24-oz.) bag frozen
Tater Tots

4 cups salsa

2 cups shredded cheese
(cheddar or Monterey
Jack), divided

12 eggs

Cook the sausage. Drain and set aside to cool. Break cooled sausage links into pieces. In a greased slow cooker, place a layer of tots, sausage, salsa, and 1½ cups of the cheese. Pour the eggs over top. Cook on high 2½ hours or until it is set and eggs are cooked. Top with remaining cheese.

Overnight Oatmeal

So creamy and wholesome, this dish is the perfect start to the day!

2 cups old-fashioned or
steel-cut oats

4 cups milk

1 cup water

½ tsp. salt

raisins (optional)

Place all the ingredients into the slow cooker and mix well. Cook on low about 6 hours.

Brenda Stanley

Florentine Breakfast Casserole

I love the combination of fresh spinach and mushrooms.

1½ cups shredded cheddar cheese

1 (9-oz.) package fresh spinach, chopped

1 cup cubed white bread

1 cup sliced fresh mushrooms

½ cup sliced green onions

6 eggs

1½ cups milk

½ cup heavy cream

1 tsp. salt

1 tsp. black pepper

1 tsp. garlic powder

Lightly grease the slow cooker. Layer ½ of the cheddar cheese and the spinach, bread, mushrooms, and green onions in bottom of the slow cooker. Whisk together the eggs, milk, cream, salt, pepper, and garlic powder. Pour egg mixture over top of everything in slow cooker. Sprinkle the remaining cheese on top. Cook on high about 2 hours.

Eggs, Ham, and Hash Browns

A full hearty breakfast—ready right when you wake up.

1 onion, chopped

1 green bell pepper, chopped

1 Tbsp. olive oil

1 (32-oz.) bag frozen hash brown potatoes

2 cups cooked cubed ham

1½ cups shredded cheddar cheese

12 eggs

1 cup milk

1 tsp. salt

½ tsp. pepper

Sauté the onion and the green pepper in hot oil until tender. Place ⅓ of the frozen hash brown potatoes in a lightly greased slow cooker. Add ⅓ of the ham, onion, green pepper, and cheese. Repeat layers, ending with cheese. In a large bowl, beat together the eggs, milk, and seasonings. Pour mixture over ingredients in slow cooker. Cook on low 8–10 hours or until set.

Brenda Stanley

Apple Pudding Cake

Sweet apples surrounded by a moist cake. This is the perfect fall dessert.

2 cups sugar

1 cup oil

2 eggs

2 tsp. vanilla

2 cups unpeeled apple, cored and finely chopped

2 cups flour

1 tsp. baking soda

1 tsp. nutmeg

1 tsp. cinnamon

1 cup chopped walnuts

Beat together the sugar, oil, eggs, and vanilla. Add apple with dry ingredients and mix well. Grease a 2-pound tin can (coffee can) and flour it well. Pour batter into can, filling no more than ⅔ full. Place can in the slow cooker. Do not add water. Cover but leave cover ajar so steam can escape. Cook on high 3½–4 hours. Cake is done when top is set. Let stand in can a few minutes before tipping pudding cake out onto a plate.

Cherry Crisp

This sweet and homey dish can use any flavor of pie filling.

2 (20-oz.) cans cherry pie filling

⅔ cup brown sugar

½ cup quick-cooking oats

½ cup flour

⅓ cup butter, softened

Lightly butter the slow cooker. Place cherry pie filling in the slow cooker. Combine dry ingredients and mix well. Cut in butter with a pastry cutter or fork. Sprinkle crumbs over the cherry pie filling. Cook on low 5 hours.

Lemon Sponge

Tart and sweet and melt-in-your-mouth good.

1 cup sugar

¼ cup flour

¼ tsp. salt

¼ cup lemon juice

1 Tbsp. lemon zest

3 eggs, separated

1 Tbsp. butter, melted

1 cup milk

1 Tbsp. powdered sugar

Mix together sugar, flour, and salt. Stir in lemon juice, lemon zest, egg yolks, butter, and milk. In a separate bowl, beat egg whites until stiff peaks form; fold into lemon mixture. Pour into a greased bowl and cover tightly with aluminum foil (secure with an elastic band). Place bowl in the slow cooker and pour in enough water to come 1 inch up sides of bowl. Cover and cook on high 4–5 hours or until topping is set and light and fluffy. Sift powdered sugar over sponge before serving.

Baked Apples

An old-fashioned favorite with the convenience of the slow cooker.

4 large apples, cored
and unpeeled

1 tsp. cinnamon

¼ cup brown sugar

4 Tbsp. butter

Place the apples in the slow cooker. Combine cinnamon and brown sugar. Stuff the mixture into the core of the apples. Top each apple with 1 tablespoon butter. Cook on low 4–5 hours.

Brenda Stanley

Pineapple Upside-Down Cake

A wonderfully simple way to make a family favorite.

½ cup butter, melted

1 cup brown sugar

1 (16-oz.) can pineapple slices, drained, reserving juice

6–8 maraschino cherries

1 (16.5-oz.) box yellow cake mix, dry

Mix together the butter and brown sugar. Spread over bottom of a greased slow cooker. Add pineapple slices and place cherries in the center of each one. Prepare cake mix according to package directions, using pineapple juice in place of part of the water. Pour cake batter over top of pineapple slices. Cover slow cooker with two tea towels and then with its own lid. Cook on high 1 hour and then turn slow cooker down to low for 3–4 hours.

Apple Crisp Crunch

A super easy dessert that is sweet and crunchy.

4 medium apples,
peeled and sliced

¼ cup honey

1 tsp. cinnamon

2 Tbsp. butter, melted

2 cups granola cereal

Place apples in a lightly greased slow cooker. Mix together honey, cinnamon, melted butter, and cereal. Spread on top of apples. Cook on low 6–8 hours.

Brenda Stanley

Berry Bread Pudding

Rich and decadent, this dish could be used for breakfast, brunch, or dessert!

6 cups cubed dense
white bread

1 cup fresh raspberries

2 cups heavy cream

2 cups milk

1¼ cups sugar

6 eggs

1 Tbsp. vanilla

Layer half of the cubed bread in a well-greased slow cooker, and sprinkle with half of the berries over top. Repeat the layers, ending with berries. Whisk together the cream, milk, sugar, eggs, and vanilla. Pour into the slow cooker over the bread cubes and berries, and gently push down the bread to evenly moisten. Cook on high about 2–3 hours or until a knife inserted in the center comes out clean. Remove the lid and cook another 15 minutes. Serve with whipped cream, milk, or ice cream.

Creamy Rice Pudding

One of my all-time favorite comfort foods.

4 cups milk

½ cup sugar

½ cup uncooked medium-grain rice (not instant)

½ cup raisins

½ tsp. ground cinnamon

Mix together the milk, sugar, and rice in the slow cooker. Cook on high 3–3½ hours, stirring occasionally. Stir in raisins and cinnamon. Pudding will thicken as it cools.

Brenda Stanley

Hot Fudge Cake

It's a molten flow of rich chocolate! There are few things more decadent!

1¾ cups brown sugar, divided

2 cups flour

¼ cup plus 3 Tbsp. unsweetened cocoa powder, divided

2 tsp. baking powder

1 tsp. salt

1 cup milk

¼ cup butter, melted

1 tsp. vanilla

3½ cups water, boiling

Mix together 1 cup brown sugar, flour, 3 tablespoons cocoa powder, baking powder, and salt. Mix in milk, butter, and vanilla until well blended. Pour into the slow cooker. Mix together remaining ¾ cup brown sugar and ¼ cup cocoa powder in a small bowl. Sprinkle evenly over mixture in the slow cooker. Pour the boiling water over top without stirring. Cook on high about 2 hours or until toothpick inserted into center comes out clean. Let it cool about 10 minutes before serving.

"Wishing to be friends is quick work, but friendship is a slow ripening fruit."

—Aristotle

Index

Index

THE ZUCCHINI HOUDINI

OVER 100 DELICIOUS RECIPES

SALADS
SOUPS
BREADS
DESSERTS
AND MORE!

BRENDA STANLEY

Brenda Stanley is a former television news anchor and investigative reporter for the NBC affiliate in eastern Idaho. She has been recognized for her writing by the Scripps Howard Foundation, the Hearst Journalism Awards, the Idaho Press Club, and the Society of Professional Journalists. She is the author of four other books—three novels and one cookbook. Brenda is an adjunct professor at Idaho State University in the Mass Communication department. She is a graduate of Dixie College in St. George, Utah, and the University of Utah in Salt Lake City. She is the mother of five grown children, including two sets of twins (born twenty months apart—yes, four kids under the age of two), and she is now a grandma. Brenda and her husband, Dave, a veterinarian, live on a small ranch near the Snake River with their horses, sheep, chickens, and dogs.